Dedicated to the children of today,
the designers of tomorrow.

Parent's Introduction

We Both Read is the first series of books designed to invite parents and children to share the reading of a story by taking turns reading aloud. This "shared reading" innovation, which was developed with reading education specialists, invites parents to read the more complex text and story line on the left-hand pages. Then, children can be encouraged to read the right-hand pages, which feature text written for a specific early reading level.

Reading aloud is one of the most important activities parents can share with their child to assist them in their reading development. However, *We Both Read* goes beyond reading *to* a child and allows parents to share the reading *with* a child. *We Both Read* is so powerful and effective because it combines two key elements in learning: "modeling" (the parent reads) and "doing" (the child reads). The result is not only faster reading development for the child, but a much more enjoyable and enriching experience for both!

You may find it helpful to read the entire book aloud yourself the first time, then invite your child to participate in the second reading. In some books, a few more difficult words will first be introduced in the parent's text, distinguished with **bold lettering**. Pointing out, and even discussing, these words will help familiarize your child with them and help to build your child's vocabulary. Also, note that a "talking parent" icon ⟲ precedes the parent's text, and a "talking child" icon ⟲ precedes the child's text.

We encourage you to share and interact with your child as you read the book together. If your child is having difficulty, you might want to mention a few things to help him. "Sounding out" is good, but it will not work with all words. Children can pick up clues about the words they are reading from the story, the context of the sentence, or even the pictures. Some stories have rhyming patterns that might help. It might also help them to touch the words with their finger as they read, to better connect the voice sound and the printed word.

Sharing the *We Both Read* books together will engage you and your child in an interactive adventure in reading! It is a fun and easy way to encourage and help your child to read—and a wonderful way to start them off on a lifetime of reading enjoyment!

New Car Design
We Both Read® Book

Dedicated to the children of today,
the designers of tomorrow.

Published by Treasure Bay, Inc.
P.O. Box 119
Novato, CA 94948 USA

Printed in Singapore

Library of Congress Catalog Card Number: 2009930963

Hardcover ISBN: 978-1-60115-243-5
Paperback ISBN: 978-1-60115-244-2

We Both Read® Books
Patent No. 5,957,693

Visit us online at:
www.webothread.com

PR-1-12

New Car Design

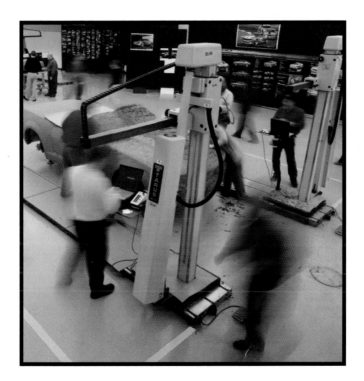

By Peter Economy

TREASURE BAY

Chances are that you rode in a car today. Maybe someone drove you to school, or maybe your dad took you to soccer or ballet practice. Perhaps you went with your mom on a quick trip to the grocery store. You might have even **traveled** by car to another city to visit your grandparents.

Not so long ago, there weren't any cars at all. Most people walked to school and to the store. If they **traveled** to another city, they went by horse or train. People wanted a faster and easier way to get where they wanted to go.

Creative people began looking for ways to satisfy this need, and in 1885 the very first car was invented.

This first car, created in Germany by a man named Karl Benz, looked very different from cars today. His **invention** had only three wheels and no top. No one had seen anything like it, and people came from miles away just to look at it.

The **PASSING** of the **HORSE**

THE silent horse power of this runabout is measurable, dependable and spontaneous. The horse power generated by supplies of hay and oats is variable, uncertain and irresponsive.

There is "*Nothing to watch but the road*" when you drive

The Oldsmobile

"*The best thing on wheels*"

You see them everywhere—Doctors, Lawyers and Merchants find the Oldsmobile the most practical vehicle for business purposes. Ladies and children can readily understand its mechanism. Unvarying reliability proves it is built to run *and does it*.

Price $650⁰⁰

Selling agencies are established in all the larger cities, where you will be gladly accorded the privilege of trying the Oldsmobile on the road. Write for illustrated book to Dept. G.

Olds Motor Works

OFFICES, Detroit, Mich.
FACTORIES—Detroit and Lansing

Soon many people wanted to buy this new **invention**. Different models of cars were created by a growing number of new car companies. As more people bought cars, fewer people rode on horses and in horse-drawn wagons and buggies. Cars were becoming faster than horses—and they did not need to eat oats!

Another creative man, named Henry Ford, built his first car in 1896. It was called a Quadricycle. Instead of using a wheel to steer, this car used a long, curved piece of metal.

At that time, cars were very expensive to buy. Usually, only wealthy people could afford to buy cars. Then in 1908, Henry Ford designed a car called the Model T. This car was more affordable because it cost less to build. This was due to Ford's innovation of the "**assembly** line."

Instead of one person building an entire car, each worker on the line worked on one part of the car. Soon most cars were built using an **assembly** line. Today, **assembly** lines are used to build almost everything we buy. However, it is now very common for **assembly** to be done by machines instead of people.

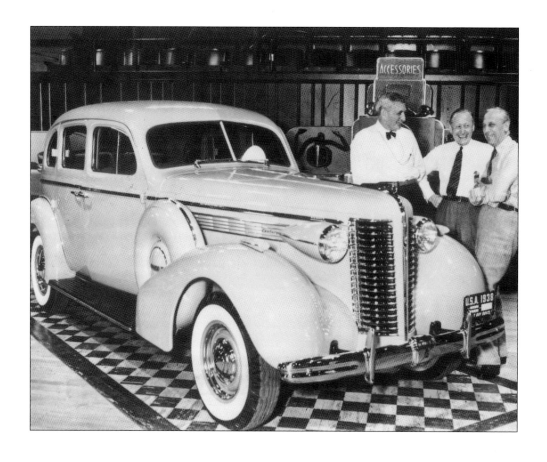

All of the Model T cars that Ford built were painted black. The Model T didn't cost a lot, but many people wanted something more exciting to drive. This led to the formation of a new car company called General Motors. Under the guidance of a man named Alfred Sloan, the company **designed** new and innovative cars.

General Motors **designed** cars that had style and power. The cars were also made in lots of different colors. Some even came in two colors! Soon General Motors was selling more cars than Ford's company.

 Today, people look for many different **features** in their cars. A lot of people look for cars that create less pollution and use less gasoline or no gasoline at all. Other people, such as racecar drivers, want cars that can go fast.

Families often want cars that can carry many people. Comfort and safety are also important **features**. Car companies must think about all of these things when they are creating new cars.

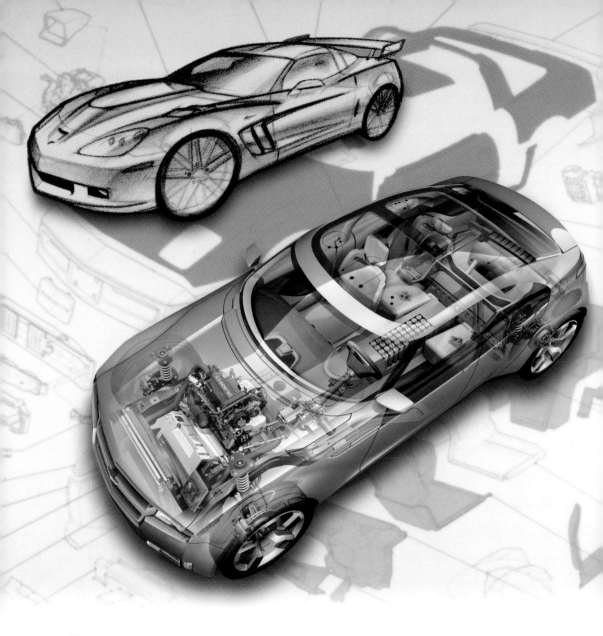

To help them find ways to satisfy the needs of their customers, car companies hire specially trained workers called **designers**. These creative people think of new and better ways to build a car. Most professional car **designers** have a college degree in industrial design.

They often start by drawing their ideas on paper. Then the ideas and drawings are turned into a computerized model.

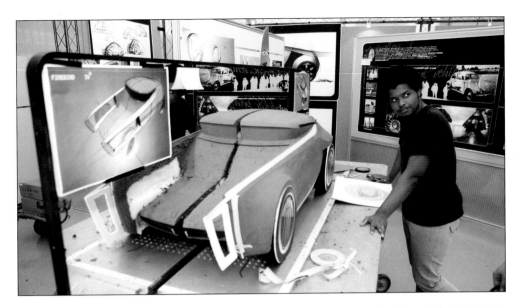

Next, a small model of the car is made. Then a full-size model is created out of clay—just like the clay you use in school for art projects.

Designers may come up with hundreds of ideas before they find one that a car company will decide to build.

Working in teams, designers experiment with innovative ideas to meet the demands of modern car buyers.

Since car companies know that people want affordable cars that cause less **pollution** and use less gasoline, many design teams are experimenting with new ways to build clean-burning engines.

The engines used in cars have hundreds of parts. The people who design engines are always looking for new ways to build stronger and lighter engines that cause less **pollution** and save energy.

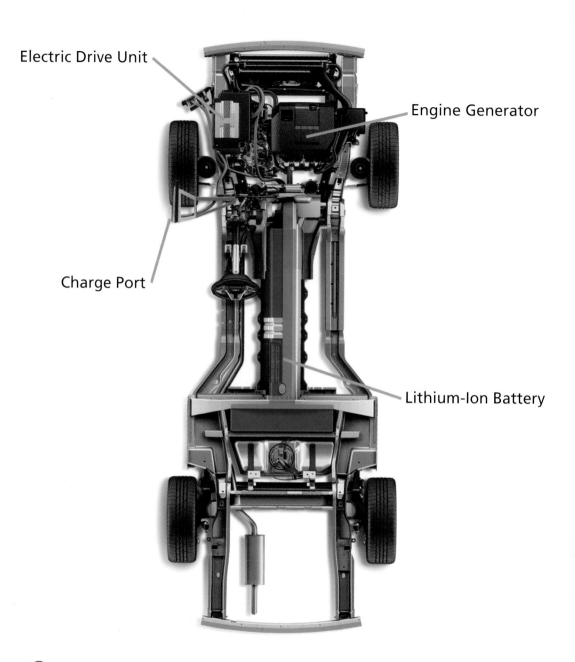

Electric Drive Unit

Engine Generator

Charge Port

Lithium-Ion Battery

Some cars just run on electricity from batteries. Their batteries are recharged when the cars are plugged into wall sockets. Other cars are hybrids. These cars run on both electricity and gas. There are even cars that use power from hydrogen, an odorless gas that does not pollute the environment.

   All of the new cars we drive today pollute much less than older cars. Hopefully car designers will find a way to make cars that don't cost a lot to build, don't cost a lot to run, and don't pollute at all.

Some designers specialize in designing **racecars**. Professional **racecar** drivers in NASCAR or the Indianapolis 500 need cars that go very fast. They also need cars that are extremely reliable and won't break down over long distances. That's why ideas for many car improvements are first tried out in **racecars**. Some of these new ideas find their way into cars like the ones you ride in with your friends or family.

Sometimes during a race, a **racecar** needs to make a "pit stop." The car is driven into a pit where a team of people changes the **racecar**'s worn out tires and fills up the car with enough gas to win the race.

      Speed, safety, and fuel efficiency are important to car buyers. But people still want a car that looks good!

      One person might want a snazzy sports car, while someone else might want a family-friendly minivan. Designers can give a car a unique personality by making a car look friendly and approachable or muscular and **aggressive**. Most car companies sell many different kinds of cars to attract different kinds of car buyers.

Ideas for the look of a car can be based on just about anything. For example, the designers might want a car to suggest the look and feel of a wild animal. To do this, they might design the headlights to look like **aggressive** eyes. And they might make the opening under the front bumper look like a mouth with teeth.

 Car designers often specialize in working on certain systems or design elements. While one team designs the interior of the car, another team designs the engine, while still another designs the exterior. A designer can spend hours or even days designing something as simple, but **important**, as a new steering wheel.

When designers create the inside of a car, they make sure it looks good and it is safe. Everything has to feel right and work right. It is also **important** that it doesn't cost too much to make the car.

Designers can't be sure that people will like their design until they have the opportunity to show it to the public. So, sometimes they create what is called a "**concept** vehicle." This special car is displayed at auto shows to get the reaction of potential car buyers. If there's a long line to see their **concept** car, the designers know they did a good job.

 Most car shows have at least a few **concept** cars displayed. They are very popular with visitors. Even if you have never been to a car show, you might have seen a concept car on television or in the newspaper.

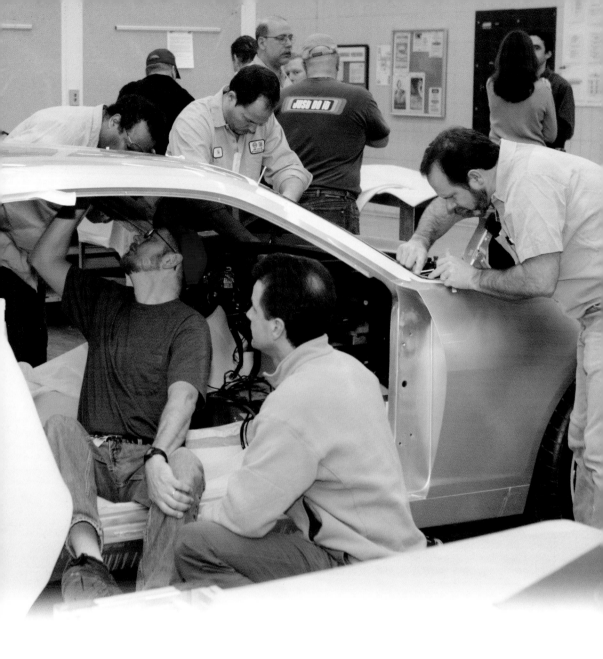

Engineers help turn the designers' ideas and concepts into actual cars. They must make sure these newly designed cars can be manufactured and assembled at a reasonable cost. They also make sure the cars will work well and be safe on the road.

The people who design and build a car are a team, just like a baseball or football team. Each person has a job, and they all work together to create a car that people will want to buy.

   After all of a car's parts are designed and engineered, a few sample cars are put together—often by hand—to be tested.

Car designs are often tested in a wind tunnel to see how the lift and drag of air will affect the movement of the car. This is called the "aerodynamics" of the car.

   The lift and drag on a car can affect how much gas it uses. A car that is shaped like an egg would probably use less gas than a car shaped like a box. However, a car shaped like a box might hold more people.

 Cars go through many tests in all kinds of conditions to be sure the designers have designed a car that is safe and reliable. Cars should be able to last for many thousands of miles of driving. Test cars are driven in the desert, in the snow, in the rain, on bumpy roads, and on smooth roads—and sometimes entirely off road.

There are men and women who have the job of test-driving cars. They drive the new cars for many hours to see if they have any problems. The designers need to fix any problems before more cars are built in the factory.

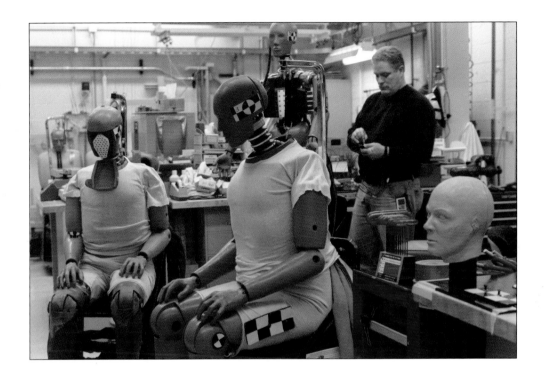

Designers also need to know if a car and the people in it will be safe and protected from harm if it crashes or is in an accident. Car manufacturers use crash-test dummies to get the test information they need for their designers.

The use of crash-test dummies have helped in many car-safety improvements, including better seat belts, collapsible steering wheels, padded dashboards, airbags, and headrests.

Some testing, like driving a car into a wall or crashing it into another car, is too dangerous for people to do safely. Crash-test dummies help designers make cars safer while making sure that no one gets hurt testing them.

 After a company decides to produce a car for sale to the public, it is built in a huge factory. Assembly lines take cars from station to station in the factory. Specially trained workers install parts at each station until the car is complete. Some of the workers aren't people at all—they are robots!

Robots do a lot of the work that people used to do to build a car. Some robots lift heavy pieces and put them in the right place. Other robots weld metal pieces onto the car using very high heat.

 Cars are available in almost every color you can imagine. The most popular colors for cars in the United States are white, black, silver, red, gray, and blue.

Because people want to be sure that the car manufacturing process does not harm the Earth, some car companies are finding ways to use less harmful paints to help protect the environment.

 Big trucks or special trains carry cars from the factory to car dealers across the country. New cars end up at your local car dealer, where your parents may have bought the car that they drive today.

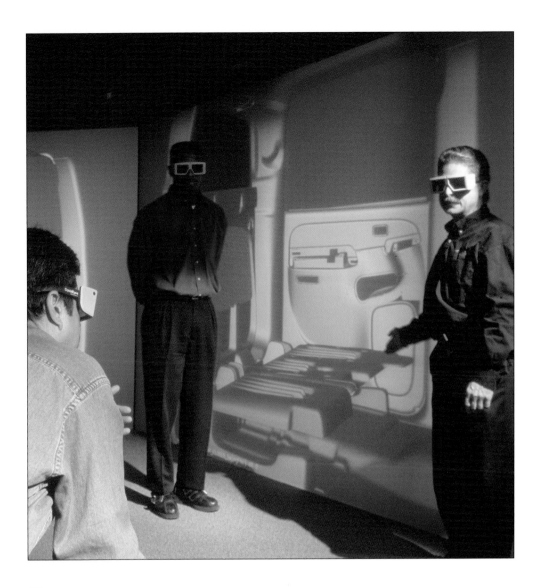

Because the needs and desires of people are always changing, car designers and engineers continue to create new ideas for cars that are faster, more reliable, safer, and more fuel efficient. New technologies, such as better batteries for electric cars, can often lead to design improvements for new cars. Designers can also improve the way they work by using new technologies, such as a virtual reality studio that allows them to see the parts they are designing in 3D.

They also keep an eye on new trends in fashion and other popular products. These clues help them as they try to figure out what people might look for next in a new car.

Would you like to design a car? You can! Just grab a pencil and some paper and start to draw. Think about the purpose of the car. Should it be fast? Should it hold a lot of people? Think about what you like and don't like about cars you see. Draw different kinds of cars to see which ones you like the best.

Who knows? Maybe the car you draw today will end up being a car of the future!

If you liked *New Car Design*, here is another
We Both Read® book you are sure to enjoy!

Soccer!

Discover exciting new information about one of the most popular sports in the world! See how games like soccer have been played for thousands of years. Learn about Pelé and Mia Hamm, two of the best soccer players ever! There are even tips on playing soccer. You might learn a new practice drill or a new way to improve your own soccer skills!